COFFEE

AND

CANNABIS

Compiled by Ann Nelson, alive in Denver.
I can't sleep so I make coffee.
Find me on Twitter:
@Philosopher's Stoned

Copyright @2018
The scanning, uploading and distribution of the contents of
this publication via the Internet or any other means is
perfectly **okay by me,** without prior written permission.
Blaze free.

INTRODUCTION

If you can improve the silence, keep it funny or interesting. And actually…just keep it funny. The world is as it seems. Coffee and cannabis will help. Keep on thinking free.

Coffee encourages happiness, good moods, comfort, clear thinking and great-heartedness. It energizes and allows you to share your elevated energy with everyone. Humans love coffee, need coffee and enjoy coffee.

"For centuries, cannabis has been used as a self-prescribed remedy for the terminal disease known as 'being alive.'" (steve carell)

"Here's my secret: I don't mind what happens." (krishnamurti)

"Here's to the stoners who could use a blunt right about now." (@Ismokeit)

Advice from Abraham:

"Make lists of positive aspects. Make lists of things you love — and never complain about anything. And as you use those things that shine bright and make you feel good as your excuse to give your attention and be who you are; you will tune to who-you-are, and the whole world will begin to transform before your eyes. It is not your job to transform the world for others—but it is your job to transform it for you. A state of appreciation is our Connection to Source where there is no perception of lack."

What the world wants from us is for us to be happy; the happiest versions of ourselves. This is our mission. This is why we are here. Here's why:

"The noblest art is that of making others happy."

p.t. barnum

To kids who are confused about what's going on, let me help you understand:

Death Eaters are completely in control of the Ministry.

brian mcElhaney

Here's to the crazy ones, the misfits, the rebels, the troublemakers, the round pegs in the square holes; the ones who see things differently. They're not fond of rules.
You can **quote** them, disagree with them, but the only thing you can't do is ignore them, because they change things. And while some may see them as the crazy ones, we see **genius**, because the ones who are crazy enough to think that they can change the world are the ones who do.

steve jobs

Everyone is born a **genius**, but the process of living de-geniuses them.

buckminster fuller

If you would be a real seeker after truth,
it is necessary that at least once in your
life you doubt, as far as possible,
all things.

rene descartes

You didn't come here to make the choice.
You've already made it.
You're here to try
to understand why you made it.

the oracle
The Matrix

When that first cup of coffee touches your soul…

coffeememes

May your coffee kick in before reality does.

@MyCoffeeHut

After a long day of not working; I like to come home, curl up by the fire with a good book, smoke some weed, throw the book on the fire and play some video games.

doug benson

I love having coffee with my mary jane.
I get so blissfully excited.

@oregon stoned thoughts

"Of course I know how to roll a joint."

martha stewart

Just a coffee, smokes, beer and books guy; stuck in a unicorn, frappuccino, vape, appletini and kindle world.

@NotZaphod

Imagine you were an alien who lived a
million years, and you got to be human —
but only for 80 years or so…

@existentialcoms

George Washington, man,
he was in a cult,
and the cult was into *aliens*.

Dazed and Confused

What if you're the only actual living person
in the universe and everyone else is just programmed to act like they're human?

@troll.me
#youmightbehigh

"And, no, I'm not an alien…but I used to be one."

elon musk

I'm automatically going to consider the possibility of an individual being a robot if they don't drink coffee.

cameron spear

Today's to-do list:
— get out of bed
— find coffee
— pretend to be human

@MyCoffeeHut

"How many cups of coffee have you had?"

—"None."

"How many?"

—"Five!"

Lorelei
Gilmore Girls

How do I take my coffee?
Seriously. Very seriously.

HomeGrounds

Weed is fat free, sugar free, preservative free, gluten free, vegan, and I'm pretty sure it grows where rainbows touch the ground.

@onlyastoner

I literally just told my dealer to make me weed-kale chips instead of weed brownies because I'm that committed to fitness right now.

@andiemain

Everyone's always telling me how great exercise is but I just went on a run and guess what it sucked.

@shut up, mike

I enjoy a good runner's high — minus the running part.

@brother sal

Me: *uncontrollable sobbing*

"I can't see you anymore. I won't let you hurt me again."

Trainer: "It was a sit-up. You did one sit-up."

@JediCheesyGrits

My go-to coffee creamer is 2 bars of xanax.

@James

AVOCADO: "Hello, I'm good fat!"

BACON: *lights cigarette*
　　　　　punches avocado

@Markydoodoo

They may take away my sugar, alcohol,
dairy, greens and beans but they shall
never take away my coffee!

I'll quit coffee.
It won't be easy drinking
my Bailey's straight,
but I'll get used to it.
It'll still be the best part of waking up.

megan mullally
Will and Grace

Longest order at Starbucks:

Double ristretto venti half-soy nonfat decaf organic chocolate brownie iced vanilla double-shot gingerbread frappucino extra hot with foam whipped cream upside down double blended, one sweet 'n low and one nutra sweet, and ice.

I hate myself a little more every time I say 'no whip' when getting coffee.

@Hufflepuff in D buff

Me: I'm into fitness
Trainer: not again
Me: fitness whole pizza in my mouth
Trainer: you should go
Me: this isn't going to "workout"
Trainer: leave now.

@Apathetic activist

I got kicked out of yoga class because I was too good.

stephen colbert

Why are you staring at me? Like you've never seen someone eat three Slim Jims
on her yoga mat before class.

@Ashley Quite Frankly

So, I'm starting to think the
cheeseburger diet
I read about online wasn't real.

@Funny Fat Guy

Why are bookstores not serving pie,
why don't libraries have baristas, and
why aren't there any doctors who tell
you to go heal in a garden?

@Lovely Filters

"Starbucks is an evil corporation that abuses coffee growers in Ethiopia...I will have a venti iced skinny cinnamon dolce latte with soy milk, no whip, one scoop of whey protein, well-mixed with cinnamon on top."

I can't wait for the barista at Starbucks to find out we've been going steady for six weeks.

@the sober irishman

Apparently "Just fuck me up" is not a proper coffee order at Starbucks.

@chrisimpossiblefilms

Hit me with your best pot…

@lori glass co

I'll have a cafe mocha vodka marijuana latte to go, please.

Half the day, I wonder if it's too late for **coffee**,

the other half I wonder if it's too early for **alcohol**.

The Funny beaver.com

Coffee: you're on the bench

Alcohol: suit up

Beats.the.Hell.out.of.me.

I once tweeted it was too early for alcohol
and I had 30 unfollows, 5 blocks
and a death threat.

@Just Joey

I can't decide if I need a hug,
a large coffee, six shots of vodka or
two weeks of sleep.

@Rebloggy

drinking my last cup of coffee for the day

Me: "It's all down hill from here."

@some copywriter

There may be coffee in his whiskey…

@the cult of mike

Today I tried to pour coffee in an
upside-down coffee mug so
happy 'Monday' to me.

morgan lewis

"Well, it's Monday," she sighed as
she poured scalding coffee on her lap
just to feel something.

@The Office Sponge

May your coffee be strong
and your Monday short.

I know what you're thinking:

"Today is going pretty well for a Monday."

…Except it's Tuesday.

@tim siedell

Before coffee, I'm a hot mess.

After: I'm a wide awake hot mess.
So there's that.

nanea hoffman

I pretend that coffee helps

but I'm still a bitch.

#justsaying

Menu:

Soup of the Day:

Coffee

@coffee lovers

First I do the coffee…then I do the stuff.

HomeGrounds

I don't always show up to work in a good mood, but when I do, every single person that comes through the door, tries to
ruin it
by being a complete asshole.

@coffeeblack

Sometimes I like coffee more than I like people.
Oh wait, that's all the time.

@Death Wish Coffee

Coffee gives me the energy I need to be mad about little things all day.

@Scotland Green

Sometimes I pretend that I don't care… but…deep down…I still don't care.

@quickmeme

To pretend, I actually do the thing:

I have therefore only
pretended to pretend.

jacques derrida

I just want someone to love and accept me
for who I pretend to be on the internet.

@neukolin hoodie

Sorry I was late for work. A guy at 7-11 put 23 creams in his coffee and I had to watch him put each one in.

@MikePrimavera

Relax, guy ordering a hot dog from 7-11 at 6:30 in the morning. No one is judging you. I'm the only one in here and you're me.

@MikePrimavera

Step aside coffee!

This morning calls for cannabis!!

Coffee enlivens the dank life.
A reason to get out of bed in the morning.

The sooner you wake up, the sooner you bake up.

@MaryJaneWanna

I silently mouth the words

"I need to get high"

at least 20 times a day.

@Ismokeit

How do you feel when there is no coffee?

depresso.

@yourlifechoices

All you need is Love…and more coffee.

mycoffeeguide.eu

I need coffee, I'm a cold coffee guy.

That's how I do.

rob riggle

I was so stoned once, I saw Ernie the Keebler elf restocking the Pecan Sandies in Spies SuperValu.

@BatShitCrazy

Smoking weed doesn't make your problems go away. It just makes you realize it's not that big of a deal.

@weed posts

I'm not fighting a spiritual war my friend, I'm smoking weed and happily walking down life's spiritual path. But…
you stay sober.

@420THC

I'm going to another dimension.
You need anything?

JRevito

You know you're high when everything you do feels like a *frakking* mission.

#sosayweall

The essential lesson I've learned in life is to just be yourself. Treasure the magnificent being that you are and recognize first and foremost you're not here as a human being only.

You're a
spiritual being having a
human experience.

wayne dyer

The treasure that is precious is the quality
of even-mindedness in all situations.

sai baba

"Be strong" I whisper to my coffee.

There was only one catch and that was Catch-22. Orr would be crazy to fly more missions and sane if he didn't, but if he was sane he had to fly them. If he flew them he was crazy and didn't have to; but if he didn't want to he was sane and had to.

joseph heller
Catch-22

Scientists have calculated that the
chances of something so patently
absurd actually existing are
millions to one.
But magicians have calculated that
million-to-one chances
crop up nine times out of ten.

terry pratchett

I'm basically David Blaine if he
didn't know magic.

@boredom daily

If my calculations are correct, when
this baby hits 88 miles per hour,
you're gonna
see some serious shit.

#backtothefuture

Any minute now the caffeine will kick in…

…any minute.

coffeememes

BAZINGA!

Waaaay too much coffee!

Imgflip

The world is hell but coffee is forever.

@LovelyFilters

The seventh circle of hell is not finding a quiet place to drink your coffee.

@LovelyFilters

The hottest places in hell are reserved for those who, in times of great moral crisis, maintain their neutrality.

Dante

Happy 4/20 to my high school guidance counselor. I turned out fine and you're reading this from the bowels of hell.

@MikePrimavera

It's like the coffee to wake up the
mind-body connection.
When I notice it
is working, depending on the dosage,
time seems to be slowing down a bit,
everything seems covered with a layer
of extra significance.

martin schirp

Being "awake" isn't cool.

It means having to dumb down 98% of your conversations everyday so you don't sound like a lunatic.

dave chappelle

Life happens.

Coffee helps.

A DAY WITHOUT COFFEE IS LIKE…

Just kidding. I have no idea.

@MyCoffee Hut

A day without coffee is like frantically trying to relax.

Do jokes help? No.

Do they hurt?

Only when they're good.

@Nein Quarterly

Some people just need a high-five…
In the face.
With a chair.
Who wants bong rips and coffee?

high times

Anytime is coffee time.

I don't think the truth is out there anymore, Mulder.

@foggymemory

Mulder: it's going to *kill us* and we can't do anything about it!

Scully: that's the sun, Mulder. you do this every day.

@DothTheDoth

Today I will drink a normal amount of coffee. I will not tap dance to fill awkward silences.
I will not scream when a bird flies overhead.

@bombsydoll

Your instant coffee was a punishment for a person in too much of a hurry.

alan watts

I put instant coffee in a microwave and almost went back in time.

steven wright

Establish psychological ascendancy
by keeping it weird.

@awayfromdivine

PROCAFFEINATING (v.):
The tendency to not start anything until
you've had a coffee.

@buffer

I put my symptoms into WebMD and it turns out I just have kids.

@sarcastic mommy

pulls lighter from bra

lights smoke

"Where's the shit you made me at school?"

@debon7

Why is the sun yelling at me?

—me, with a hangover.

@bubbles n' booze

takes a long drag from a cigarette
points at your baby
"What's wrong with your dog?"

@Wunder Zoda

Scientists in London are working on a substitute for alcohol that doesn't cause hangovers. When asked what they're calling it, the scientists said: "weed."

jimmy fallon

Drugs and alcohol is not the answer. Unless you're asking what I'm doing this weekend.

quickmemes

*I have lost the way in
and the way out.
I have lost the earth, the
moon and the sky.
Don't put another cup of
wine in my hand,
pour it in my mouth,
I've lost the way to my mouth.*

rumi

#ican'tfeelmyfacewheni'mwithyou

Last googled:

"Things to care about."

@onlyastoner

burglar gently waking me

"You live like this?!?"

@ericsshadow

Step aside coffee!

This morning calls for cannabis!!

Medicated and Motivated

Cheech: Hey man, did he say he's got bricks of Columbian?

Chong: Coffee man. Coffee. Pay attention.

Ironically, the best way for me to remember something I just forgot is to forget about trying to remember it.

mark normans
#youmightbehigh

What's so great about remembering stuff?

nathan caton

I live on Earth at present, and
I don't know what I am.
I know that I am not a category.
I am Not a thing — a noun.
I seem to be a verb,
an evolutionary process —
an integral function of universe.

buckminster fuller

God is a verb.

buckminster fuller

Always remember that you are
absolutely unique.
Just like everyone else.

margaret mead

Solitude: being alone

Loneliness: thinking that other people
are not.

@the dead author

Dear Diary:

coffee.

@LovelyFilters

This era of string theory and god particles is cool af but right now I just need some peace and quiet to drink my coffee and read my book.

@trajectory unknown

If you need me, I'll be pivoting. From impotent rage to quiet desperation.

@Nein Quarterly

I put Redbull in my coffee this morning instead of water and now I can see noises.

@rebeccacade

I've got 99 problems and
cannabis coffee
solved like 86 of them.

@Pot-o-Coffee

Just made a cup of coffee for myself,

took a sip and said "Thank you!"

Not sure why.

@mindflakes

Kierkegaard pointed out that we live moving forward, but attempt understanding by looking back.

@New Philosopher

I like my men like I like my coffee: a momentary comfort in the midst of all my suffering.

@KimKierkegaardashian

I like my coffee like I like my women: kept at a distance, emotionally, due to unconscious fears of abandonment.

@chuuch

Hi, welcome to assumptions club. I think we all know why we're here.

@MehGyver

Does anyone know where I can buy an IV bag filled with pure caffeine?

@The Real RobG

Me: want me to bring coffee up to you?

What my wife said: if you want to.

What I heard: if you want to live…

@Mr_Kapowski

I don't drink coffee to wake up.
I wake up to drink coffee.

quickmemes

You know what would make a great coffee table book? A coffee table book about coffee tables…
that turns into a coffee table.

jerry seinfeld

I'm already stoned tomorrow.

@onlyastoner

"Why is millennial humor so weird?"

It's called a resurgence of neo-dadaism, you uncultured filth. Take an art class and get depressed.

kyle, but spooky

If James Joyce wrote a book about you it would be called "Uselysses."

@boredom daily

…and the last whale, like the last man,
smoke his last pipe, and then himself
evaporates in the final puff.

herman melville
Moby Dick

A gentle reminder from the Surrealists:

It is what it is.

Unless it's a pipe.

@Nein Quarterly

It is what you read when you don't have to that determines who you will be when you can't help it.

oscar wilde

I love Moby Dick but I disagree with
its main philosophy, which is
"the ocean is cool."

@JoshGrimmer

Have your Ishmael call my Ishmael.

@Nein Quarterly

Best film synopsis ever (actually in the newspaper):

The Wizard of Oz: Transported to a surreal landscape, a young girl kills the first person she meets and then teams up with three strangers to kill again.

@You Had One Job

Don't ever let anyone tell you that fairy tales aren't real. I drink a potion made from magic beans everyday, and it brings me back to life.

whisper

My blood has been replaced with dark black coffee…

@Articuno

The smarter you are
the better the drugs are.

@psychedelicdrugs

You can't complain when you've got
Mary Jane.

greenbakebox

Idealism: think, produce
Materialism: work, produce
Existentialism: put on airs, have a coffee

jan machajski

Americans spend an average of $1,092 on coffee each year.

@what the f*ck facts

"I was taken by the power that savoring a simple cup of coffee can have to connect people and create community."

howard schultz
Starbucks CEO

I want to open a coffee shop called "No Talking!"

@josh comers

I'll read my books and I'll drink coffee
and I'll listen to music,
and I'll bolt the door.

j.d. salinger

Everything's better when you're high.
If you don't smoke,
I don't know why.

cameron thomaz
the wizard of *House Khalifa*

Coffee accepts you for who you aren't.

@some copywriter

Sit back, relax and
smoke some weed.

@Ismokeit

Don't judge someone until you have

shared a joint with them.

@lord vapor

Suddenly, things are just a little more bearable…

I like me better when I'm stoned.

@Stoners

Stoners smoke the sacred herb. Stoners are normally happier, less violent people who have a better appreciation for life. Stoners are good people who don't have to escape drugs by turning to reality.

bmw

I see you're trying to make a point but it's rollin right past me.

URBAN Stoner 6

The person who says it cannot be done should not interrupt the person who is doing it.

chinese proverb

WARNING:

Consumption of cannabis may cause
feelings of **euphoria,**
make music sound better and/or
inspire **creativity**.

@Greenland PDX

A genuine smile distributes the cosmic
current, Prana, to every body cell.

The happy man is less subject to disease,
for happiness actually attracts into the body
a greater supply of the universal life energy.

yogananda

Sometimes you just need to step outside,
get some fresh air, clear your head,
and remind yourself of who you are
and where you want to be.

@Mind of a Hippy

"I can't quit coughing,
I think I need some fresh air."

"We're outside."

@onlyastoner

Keep close to Nature's heart…
and break clear away, once in a while,
and climb a mountain or spend a week
in the woods.
Wash your spirit clean.

john muir

The John Denver song, *Rocky Mountain High* seems kind of prophetic at this point.

@stoned deep thoughts

I'm not a stoner, but my best friends are so when they smoke, naturally, I do too, because I'm supportive like that.

@weed humor

Study finds 2 to 3 joints per day reduces your risk of giving a shit.

@weed humor

The State of Colorado had to switch mile marker '420' to '419.99' because people kept stealing it.

Sometimes I shock myself with the smart stuff I say and do, other times I get out of the car with my seat belt on.

@High Thoughts
#how high are you?

I just spent 15 minutes searching for my phone in the car, while using my phone as a torch.

soho wedding.com
#you're fucking high

I love how coffee tricks me into thinking
I'm in a good mood for about 27 minutes.

someecards

You would have to smoke about
1500 pounds of bud
in less than 15 minutes
to overdose on cannabis.

@IAmSoBaked

Ordinary life does not interest me,
I seek only the **high** moment.

anais nin

The cello.
Because the violin is too small.
The bass, too low.
Wagner, too long.
And life, too short.

@Nein Quarterly

Speaking of Liszt,
he has been recognized as the official composer of the Abyss
and
Blake (you know Blake) is the poet/artist in residence.

@Basque Philosopher
#DanteSymphony
#DoorsofPerception
#DivineComedyIllustrations

We regret to inform you that autumn is for the poets.

Fall, for the rest of us.

@Nein Quarterly

Poetry remembers the old days
It was great
There was no TV
no books, novels
no magazines
It was just me and God
And I was His pencil

john guzlowski

I couldn't think of the word 'elephant'
so
I said 'hose face' in case you wondered
how my English degree is working out.

@james breakwell

I use cannabis as a writer's aid…
it is the greatest thing ever for
writer's block.

gay hendricks

Bring your thoughts to life
coz in this life
there ain't no limits,
they just made you
think that way.

@euphoria

Sometimes, I use big words I don't always fully understand in an effort to make myself sound more photosynthesis.

ingflip.com

When asked how it felt to be the smartest man alive, Albert Einstein replied:

"I don't know, you'll have to ask

Nikola Tesla."

Knowing a great deal is not the same as being smart; intelligence is not information alone but also judgment, the manner in which information is collected and used.

carl sagan

You can be educated, intelligent and still smoke marijuana.

@weed posts

Rudolph Steiner — a philosopher who believed we have lost our more primitive connection to nature. Check out your relationship with flora.

@Basque Philosopher

There is no nice way to say this —

some philosophers require wrangling.

@Basque Philosopher

Most people are other people. Their thoughts are someone else's opinions, their lives a mimicry, their passions a quotation.

oscar wilde

"I can't hear you,
I've got a banana in my ear."

ernie

Look good
Feel great
Laugh a lot
Sleep in late

Do not wait to strike till the iron is hot;
but make it hot by striking.

william butler yeats

…And they told me last night they dreamt they were me and I was holding the published copy of my novel and they don't remember the title…

@bramble witch

Are you a good witch or a bad witch?

"Depends on how much coffee there is."

We are the granddaughters of the
witches
you weren't able to burn.

tish thawer

Some women fear the fire
Some women simply become it…

r.h. sin

Not all girls are made of sugar and spice and everything nice.

Some girls are made of adventure, fine beer, brains and no fear.

@stevemaraboli.com

When choosing between two evils,
I always like to try the one I've never
tried before.

mae west

But first, coffee.

Ever realized how fucking surreal
reading a book is?
You stare at marked slices of
tree for hours on end,
hallucinating vividly.

@wordsinspire1
#you'rereadingonenow

Books and coffee just go together.

@PoemsHaven

If by club you mean reading club then,
yes,
I'll be up in the club tonight.

@boredom daily

Just told a guy talking on his phone in the library to shut the fuck up, and everyone applauded me, so I told them to shut the fuck up too.

@MikePrimavera

I think sometimes I can come off as pretentious and off-putting to people who are inferior to me and dumb.

allen s. williams

You arrive early at the office one morning to find a doppelgänger doing all your work.

Instead of confronting him, you head to the beach.

@small worlds

I don't always attract crazy people
but when I do
they're raving fuckin lunatics.

high times

Weed:

Rumored to kill brain cells… actually stimulates the growth of new brain cells.

offgridworld.com

What if being stoned is our natural state
and the marijuana only counteracts some
ever-present, mind-altering toxin
in the air?

@quickmeme

Just decided NOT to eat a hot dog that fell on the ground and that my friends is called "growing up."

brooks wheelan

What if we used to be able to make wishes…

But then someone wished we couldn't.

conspiracy keanu.com

What if the first person who ate poison berries was just allergic and we're missing out on a delicious berry?

@quickmeme

I don't know if hemp is going to save the world but its the only thing that can.

jack herer

I smoke a lot of weed when I write,
generally speaking…I don't know if it
helps me write.
It makes me not mind that I'm writing. And
I don't know if it makes me work better, but
it makes me not care that I'm working.
Who wants to work? But if you're stoned,
it doesn't seem like work.

seth rogen

I used to smoke weed.
I still do, but I used to, too.
#YFH

A new poll says a majority of americans have smoked pot.

Also, the sky is blue and water is wet.

@onlyastoner

When the world's gone mad, friends, at least you can take comfort in poetry.

@Nein Quarterly

A new report claims that
William Shakespeare
was a marijuana user and may have been
high when he wrote some of his plays.
Which explains that one line:
"To be, or not to be…wait, what was the
question?"

jimmy fallon

More recent studies have found
a relationship between
coffee and cannabis
in the same areas of the brain.

While caffeine does not measurably increase the sensitivity of the CBD receptors to THC, it does prolong their altered state to above pre-stimulation levels and makes the effects of cannabis last longer.

viewzone.com

I set my standards **high.**
Actually, I do a lot of things **high.**

culture konopna

Cannabis:

A medicine so awesome that most people take it just for the side effects.

@lord vapor

If you don't smoke weed, you'll honestly never understand why people smoke weed.

@weed humor

It's impossible to explain a color
without
saying the name of the color…

@High Thoughts

I don't always not smoke weed.
But when I do, I don't.

In high school I was voted most likely to have weird anger issues.

@ihateitmunky

Someone just said hi to me at
the gas pump,
what the fuck is their problem.

@ihateitmunky

BEE 1: You get **one** chance to sting someone, so make sure they're a threat

BEE 2: Well that guy's over there walking.

BEE 1: He's doing *WHAT??*

@Ponk

I think my new thing will be to be a
real happy guy.
I'll just walk around being real happy
until some jerk says something stupid to me.

jack handey

Weed doesn't make you happy,
it makes you realize all the things there are
to be happy about.

@Ismokeit

I am a kind of paranoiac in reverse.

I suspect people of plotting to

make me happy.

j.d. salinger

I am a happy and positive person, and fuck you if you don't like it.

@BluntCard

When I smoke I go from stressed to fuck-it real quick.

@420Humor

You have power over your mind —

not outside events.

Realize this, and you will find strength.

marcus aurelius

If this is coffee,
please buy me some tea;

but if this is tea,
please buy me some coffee.

abraham lincoln

How much coffee do you have to
drink
to become the void?

@The Circus

Sometimes you need to just say

fuck it and smoke a fat ass joint.

@IAmSoBaked

At the start of this new year, I am leaving my past behind me…so if I owe you some money, I am sorry…I have moved on.

@LindzThoughts

I listed my exe as my
emergency contact
at my new job because if I have a
heart attack I need to tell Kathy
to burn in hell one last time.

@chuuch

You will not be punished for your anger;
you will be punished by your anger.

buddha

He who controls his mind and has cut
off desire and anger realizes the Self.

bhagavad gita

Life is far too important a thing ever
to
talk seriously about it.

oscar wilde

Chuck Norris grinds his coffee with his teeth and boils water with his rage.

One minute of anger weakens the immune system for 4 to 5 hours.

One minute of laughing boosts your immune system for 24 hours.

david avocado wolfe

Yeah, I've tried adults sans coffee.

People got hurt.

@steveolivas

Me: I have chronic pain. It flares up whenever someone challenges my beliefs.

Friend: That's not really how chronic pain works.

Me: ow *owww*

@therealeatwood

Stressed, blessed
and
coffee obsessed

Why struggle to open a door
between us
when the whole wall is an illusion?

rumi

There are no mistakes,
only happy accidents.

bob ross

There are two rules for success…

1. Never reveal everything you know

The world is changed by your example,
not by your opinion.

@Sputnik Sweetheart

Ideology:

The mistaken belief that your beliefs
are neither beliefs nor mistaken.

@Nein Quarterly

Ideology always paves the way
toward atrocity.

terence mcKenna

Marijuana won't kill you, but a local police department armed by the pentagon might.

"Smoking even one marijuana cigarette is equal in brain damage to being on Bikini Island during an H-bomb blast."

ronald reagan

hold my beer…..

Let this sink in for a minute…
The government is at war with a plant,
That has never actually killed anyone,
ever…
And they're losing!

george carlin

When a well-packaged web of lies has
been sold gradually to the masses
over generations,
the truth will seem
utterly preposterous and its speaker
a raving lunatic.

dresden james

The number one reason why marijuana
is illegal is that the Pharma Cartel does
not
want you to grow your own medicine.
The Declaration of Independence was
written on hemp paper. The first car ever
made ran on hemp oil. Hemp seeds are
also the healthiest food on the planet
with
the highest protein content out of
any plant.

joe rogan

It was a high waking up in the morning
and thinking:
am I going to get arrested today,
or am I going to make $4 million?

richard stratton
editor-in-chief, *High Times*

Saying weed is a gateway drug is like saying Kool Aid leads to alcohol.

@weed humor

Caffeine.

The gateway drug.

eddie vedder

Life is like a cup of coffee.

To be filled to the brim and enjoyed with friends.

I miss the good ol' days, when being a conspiracy theorist meant you had fun theories to tell at parties…not a member of the alt-right.

amber nelson

No man delights in the bearer of bad news.

sophocles
Antigone

Imagine if you will, a country where 1% control almost all the wealth and power and the other 99% are so brainwashed, they fight vigorously to keep it that way.

rod serling
The Twilight Zone

The Nixon campaign in 1968, and the Nixon White House after that, had *two* enemies: the *antiwar Left*, and *black people.* You understand what I'm saying: We *knew* we couldn't make it illegal to be either against the war or blacks. But by getting the public to associate the **hippies with marijuana** and **blacks with heroin**, and then *criminalizing* both heavily, we could *disrupt* those communities. We could *arrest* their leaders, *raid* their homes, *break up* their meetings, and *vilify* them night after night on the evening news. *Did we know we were lying about the drugs? Of course we did.*

john ehrlichman
Assistant to President Nixon

method:

sell the lie with authority,
then change the subject to
something emotional

"We'll know
our disinformation program
is complete when
everything the American public
believes is false."

william casey
CIA Director, *1981*

A despot doesn't fear eloquent writers
preaching freedom — he fears
a drunken poet who may crack
a joke that will take hold.

e.b. white

Sounds like the beginning of a
conspiracy theory…

Everything you know is wrong

Remember sitting in history, thinking:

"If I were alive then, I would've…"

You're alive now.
Whatever you're doing
is what you would've done.

@slack2thefuture

Back during the great weed prohibition…
we had to buy our shit off the streets
illegally.

There was none of this "go down to the
head shop buy a dime bag."

@TomFoolery

…Marijuana is one of the safest, therapeutically active substances known to man.

DEA Judge Francis Young

Marijuana is one of the least toxic substances in the whole pharmacopoeia.

professor lester grinspoon
Harvard Med

Marijuana:

safer than peanuts!

The brain on marijuana will never deviate from its destined disposition, nor be driven to madness. Marijuana is a mirror reflecting man's deepest thoughts, a magnifying mirror. It's true, but only ever a mirror.

charles baudelaire, *1860*

Be curious, not judgmental.

walt whitman

I like to party, and by party I mean stay at home and smoke a lot of weed.

@stoned deep thoughts

Let's lie under the stars
and smoke a blunt.

@Ismokeit
#youdeserveit

My son and his friends are great.
They always spray the house with
air freshener before I get home.

My brain: just be cool. just be cool. just be cool…

Me: nope.
(repeat daily)

@FatherWithTwins

High people understand other
high people.
They catch things that others don't.

Cannabis tutorials.com

Can you feel the buzz of
cannabis law reform in the air,
the tide turns and soon the plant
will be freed from
the shackles of prohibition.

ancient jay

Coffee is my second favorite plant.

green flower media

You know you're a stoner when
you save food because you know
it'll taste better later when you're high.

@Ismokeit

"You're entirely bonkers,
completely off your head.
But I'll tell you a secret.
All the best people usually are."

lewis carroll

With all honesty I can tell you that very soon I'm going to get extremely high and go see CATS on Broadway.

marcus monroe

I love coffee.

10% coffee.

90% creamer.

quickmeme

You say that you love coffee.
The two cups of flavored creamer
you add tells me that is a lie.

Imgflip

In protest I'm not doing anything today

or the rest of my life.

jim gaffigan

My plan for today:

Same as always!

Drink coffee and be sexy.

I like my coffee how I like myself:
Dark, bitter and too hot for you.

tumblr.com
#jk

Girl, you must be coffee because I want you every day but you tend to give me anxiety attacks.

@michael, still here

Every human being must go through the adventure of being anxious.

It can make the biggest difference in the way your look comes together.

@Kim**Kierkegaard**ashian

The truth is a trap. You cannot get it without it getting you;
you cannot get the truth by capturing it, only by its capturing you.

soren **kierkegaard**

It is impossible to begin to learn that which one thinks one already knows.

epictetus

It is the mark of an educated mind to be able to entertain a thought without accepting it.

aristotle

Asked whether Shakespeare was really Shakespeare and skepticism about accepting that a single person was able to produce such a body of work,

Bob Dylan says:

"People have a hard time accepting anything that overwhelms them."

My only hope is to forget what I'm afraid of, and that scares me.

alec sulkin

tries new coffee with 300% more caffeine

"It's okay. Can't feel a difference."

[5 minutes later]

throws refrigerator out window

@Tmoney68

NOW

PANIC

AND

FREAK

OUT

Had the dream last night where I'm somehow taking an exam for a class I'd never attended or studied for.

ken jennings
Jeopardy

What if dreams are glimpses into the lives of our 'Selfs' in another dimension.

@High Thoughts

Shaggy: Like chill out, Scooby-Doo…
         Stop shaking.

Scooby-Doo: *Me? That's you.*

Shaggy: Oh, right it's me, sorry.

Coffee!

Is the planet shaking or is it just me?

@coffee.shaking

Sometimes a lil weed is all you need

***

99 problems and 420 solutions

If at first you don't succeed,
roll a blunt and smoke some weed.

@someecards.com

I wish people offered me weed
as much as my middle school
health teacher made it seem they would.

@High Thoughts

Dream scenario:

The year is 2030, you're sitting next to your spouse with lil kiddos and a golden retriever watching the 25 days of Christmas.

Snow is falling, the fireplace is lit and so are you.

@weed humor

Wake and bake the healthy way with

Hemp Seed Coffee!

#hippie butter hemp seeds

Sometimes life is merely a matter of
coffee
and whatever intimacy a cup of coffee affords.

richard brautigan

I'm having…

one of those honeyed afternoons

when I don't know who I am.

catie rosemary

Tis a foggy, foggy morning.
Having coffee and delighting in
paradox.

vita hall

Ever wonder why a rainbow is shaped like a dome?

Crack of dawn

sloshed with coffee.

@A Murder of Crows

My description of paradise:

This morning,
with her,
having coffee.

johnny cash

Be careful, marijuana may cause:

intelligent thought, peacefulness, bliss, love and the feeling of oneness with your surroundings.

kush and wizdom

I want to live in a universe where coffee
and people get warmer,
not colder.

@some copywriter

I wanna live life, and never be cruel,
I wanna live life, and be good to you.
I wanna fly,
And never come down,
And live my life,
And have friends around.

coldplay

The important joy for those who are awake
is to seek each other out, connect with others who are awake; talk, sing and celebrate together. This will create a groundswell of awareness.

As this groundswell increases and spreads out, it will awaken the stirring and will begin
to stir those who are still sleeping.

buckminster fuller

A good relationship should make you feel strong, productive and able to take over the world.

…oh wait. That's coffee.

Coffee does that…

@Death Wish Coffee

Coffee, a chocolate croissant and

the smell of the sea.

Coffee creates a space to be in.

vita hall

It was one of the best days I can't remember in a long time.

the Marijuana-logues

I have measured out my life
with coffee spoons.

t.s. eliot

Listening to the wind roar while sipping
a perfect cup of coffee.

Peace.

vita hall

In Endymion, I leaped headlong
into the sea, and thereby have become
better acquainted with the sounding, the
quicksands, and the rocks; than if I had
stayed upon the green shore, and piped
a silly pipe, and took tea and
comfortable advice.

john keats, *1818*

"There is no need to search; achievement leads to nowhere. It makes no difference at all, so just be happy now! Love is the only reality of the world, because it is all One, you see. And the only laws are **paradox, humor and change.** There is no problem, never was, and never will be. Release your struggle, let go of your mind, throw away your concerns, and relax into the world. No need to resist life, just do your best. Open your eyes and see that you are far more than you imagine. **You are the world**, you are the universe; you are yourself and everyone else, too! It's all the marvelous Play of God. Wake up, regain your humor. ***Don't worry, just be happy.*** You are already free!——*Socrates*

        dan millman
        Way of the Peaceful Warrior

I would trade all my technology for
one afternoon with Socrates.

steve jobs

True knowledge exists in knowing
that
you know nothing.

socrates

"Pooh," said Rabbit kindly,
You haven't any brain."

"I know," said Pooh humbly.

a.a.milne

Pour into it and it will never be filled;
pour out of it and it will never be empty.

No one knows why.

This is **Tao.**

chang-tzu

Anything I say or do before I've had my coffee doesn't count.

coffee.org

arranges pieces of the wreckage on the beach

SEND COFFEE

@some copywriter

If it weren't for the coffee,
I'd have no identifiable personality
whatsoever.

david letterman

To me, you're perfect! (yes, you)

@mitchell royel

Holden Caulfield

thinks you're a phony.

"Well, if you've got work to do, Wallace,
I don't want to interfere. I was reading
an article in the paper the other day where
a certain amount of responsibility around
the home was good character training.

Goodbye, Mr. and Mrs. Cleaver."

eddie haskell

I like coffee because it gives me the
illusion
that I might be awake.

lewis black

We are powerfully imprisoned by the
terms in which
we have been conducted to think.

buckminster fuller

It is almost impossible for you to stop thinking at any moment.

@Mind Blowing

A great many people think they are
thinking
when they are really rearranging their
prejudices.

edward r. murrow

Don't believe everything you believe

When you wash your hands, when you make a cup of coffee,
when you're waiting for the elevator —
instead of indulging in thinking,
these are all opportunities for
being there
as a still, alert presence.

eckhart tolle

I was given Eckhart Tolle's book
The Power of Now.

It's all about living in the moment
but I was too busy
living in the moment
to read it.

@tom rhodes

I'm a janitor at MIT and I see some extremely hard ass equation on the chalk board.

I quickly erase it because I'm not being paid to do math.

@mikefossey

carpin all those diems

When I get depressed, I just think of an
elephant walking into a bar.
Ordering a drink.
And trying to forget…

@Nein Quarterly

I used to think people wore sunglasses to protect their eyes from the sun.

I think the real reason is because of the harshness of reality.

@Basque Philosopher

Man looks without seeing,
listens without hearing,
touches without feeling,
eats without tasting,
moves without physical awareness,
inhales without awareness of
odor or fragrance,
and talks without thinking.

leonardo da vinci

Do you ever zone out
but you are aware that you are
zoned out
but you are just too lazy to
zone back in?

You ever have moments in life where
you think you have too much time to
think about time?

@Baked Beans
#you'refuckinhigh

The world we have created is
a product of our thinking; it cannot
be changed without
changing your thinking.

albert camus

It is our choices, Harry, that show what
we truly are, far more than our abilities.

dumbledore

There is no living thing that is not afraid
when it faces danger.

True courage is in facing danger
when you are afraid.

L. frank baum

Sometimes there is no next time,
no time-outs, no second chances.

Sometimes it's now or never.

alan bennet
#One day or day one. You decide.

Measure goals in how much coffee it took
to accomplish them.

@Death Wish Coffee

Do Lipton employees take
coffee breaks?

steven wright

Every day should be National Coffee Day.
Perk up. It's coffee o'clock.

National Coffee Day:

September 29

Sometimes.…C is for coffee.

cookie monster

Save the Earth!

It's the only planet that has coffee!

thecoffeecousins.com

The only reason I drink so much coffee
is because I don't get enough sleep
because of all the coffee I drink.

@someecards

Tripping in a dream and waking up
with a jolt is called Hypnic jerk
and happens because your brain
thinks the body is dying.

@Mind Blowing

Actual topic on YouTube:

"10 signs you may have already died"

It's weird how life can be synonymously
hard and amazing…
feeling like you're propelling forward
while being pulled back.

ryan pernofski

If there is no oxygen in space...
then how does the sun burn?

@euphoria
#YFH

I did not hear the question,
but the answer is coffee.

We are not born knowing the truth
about Cannabis.
We surely are not taught in school.
Unless we are fortunate to cross paths
with someone to enlighten us, we may be
sentenced to stumble through life unaware
of our full potential.
Cannabis unlocks so many secrets;
non-toxic pain treatment,
renewable industrial resources effective cancer
cure, sage relaxation, environmental healer,
financial renewal and so much more. The truth
needs a messenger.

MANY messengers.

bettie retro

Benefits of CBD:

eases pain
eases nausea
inspires hope
spurs creativity
alleviates arthritis
slows Alzheimer's
prevents glaucoma
decreases anxiety
slows inflammation
reduces blood sugar
stops bacteria growth
eliminates nightmares
reduces nerve damage
stimulates bone growth
improves lung capacity
prevents spread of cancer
controls epileptic seizures
suppresses muscle spasms
engenders loving thoughts
eases MS, Crohn's, strokes
Parkinsons, and PTSD
and more…
much more…

"Marijuana is medicine."

queen victoria
cannabis patient

Stoners have a chill view on life in general. They don't get themselves involved in the dramas that come along with life; take it as it goes, knows who they want to spend time with and don't mess around with other people's heads. They are straightforward, without hidden motives.

True stoners tend to be introverts, they know their values in life, and are artistic.

Stoners don't use weed as a typical drug, only to get fucked up; rather they use it as a gateway to another state of mind, an:

elevated consciousness.

Stoners usually prefer to be around other stoners because only a true stoner will understand another true stoner.

urban dictionary

Learn what is to be taken seriously
and
laugh at the rest.

herman hesse

At the height of laughter,
the universe is flung into a
kaleidoscope
of new possibilities.

jean houston

In the end,

everything is a gag.

charlie chaplin

Ducunt wolentem fata;
nolentem trahunt

*The Fates lead him who will;
he who won't, they drag*

seneca

Thinking is difficult,
that's why most people judge.

carl jung

I was really counting on the world
making more sense as I got older, but
nope.

@tim siedell

A man who stands for nothing will fall for anything.

malcolm X

The thing about smart people is that
they seem like crazy people
to dumb people.

ralph smart

I get high on intelligent conversations….

@Mind of a Hippy

Be mindful of your Self-Talk.
It's a conversation with the universe.

masterjonathanfield.com

At the center of your being you have
the answer;

you know who you are and you know
what you want.

lao tzu

Every artist dips his brush
in his own soul,
and paints his own nature
into his pictures.

henry ward beecher

"I hate quotations."

ralph waldo emerson

I know not all that may be coming,
but be it what it will,

I'll go to it laughing.

herman melville
Moby Dick

www.ingramcontent.com/pod-product-compliance
Lightning Source LLC
Chambersburg PA
CBHW051749040426
42446CB00007B/285